TO: _____

FROM: _____

DATE: _____

The Self-Care A-Z

Adult Coloring Book

Terricka Hardy, LCSW, ACSW, BCD

ISBN-13: 978-1539970361
ISBN-10: 1539970361

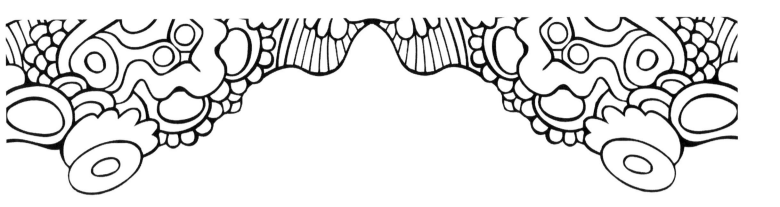

Who said self-care had to be boring?
Relax your mind and prepare to enjoy a creative journey.

Sometimes we just have to get back to the basics. Coloring is
often associated as an activity for children, however adults
benefit tremendously from this self-soothing activity.
In fact, coloring is known to reduce stress, promote creativity,
increase self-awareness, and much more. It's amazing how
the simple things can help soothe the complexities of life.
The art of coloring is both simple and calming.

Coloring puts you back in touch with the inner kid that is in us
all while promoting self-care and relaxation. Prepare to embark
on a thought provoking, yet soothing journey. Enjoy 26 fun yet
intricate coloring pages comprised of words ranging
from A to Z coupled with 26 thought provoking quotes
that will spark creativity.

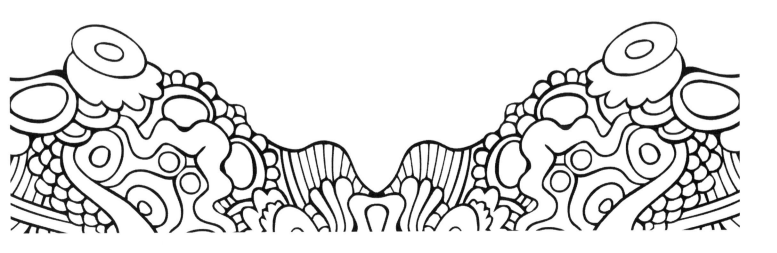

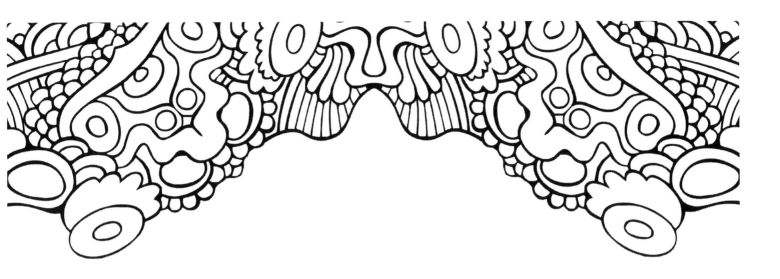

HOW TO USE THIS BOOK

There simply are NO RULES. Coloring inside of the lines,
coloring outside of the lines, and even scribbling
are all welcomed. Allow the empowering quotes and
intricate designs to inspire the creativity within.

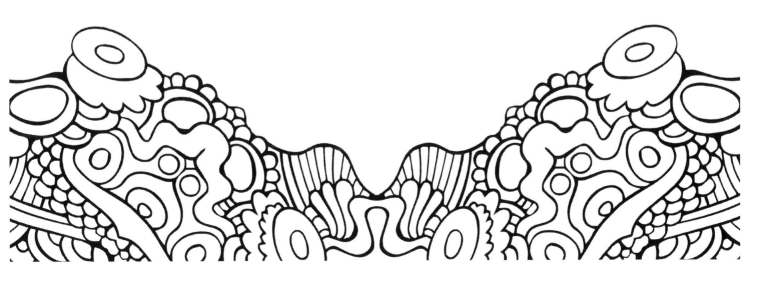

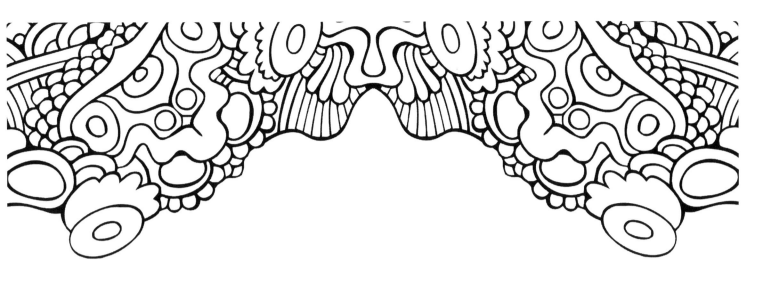

APPRECIATION

Appreciation is the foundation of self-care.

When you learn to appreciate the things you currently have

in life you'll realize just how rich you are.

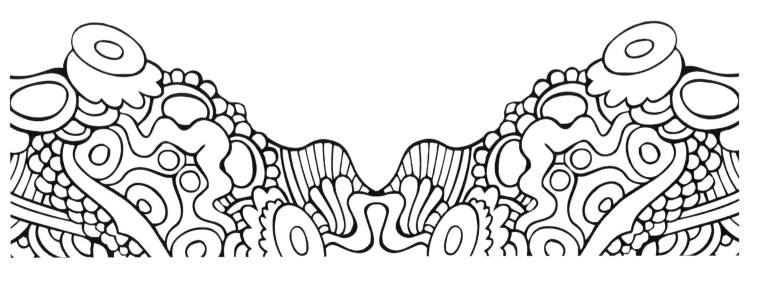

APPRECIATION

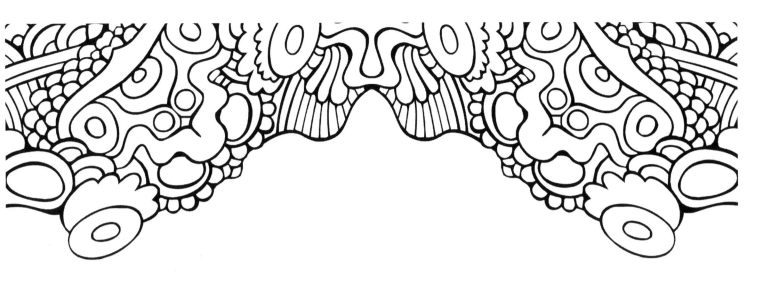

BALANCE

Balance just doesn't happen; you must create it.

The secret to balance is learning to make more

deposits into your life than withdrawals.

Create your own balance.

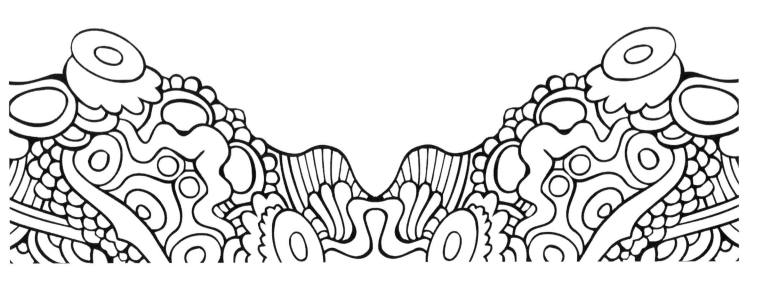

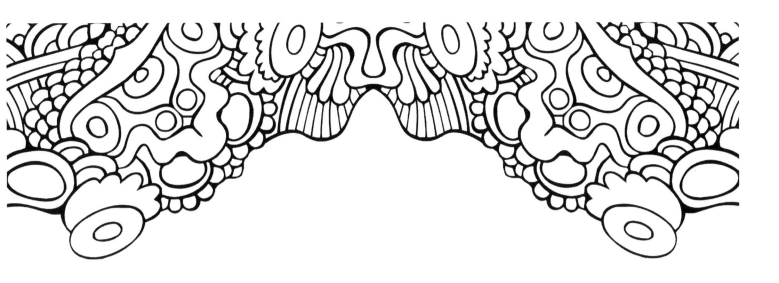

CALM

Amid chaos, you have the power to create your personal place of calmness. Where there is power there is calmness. Relinquish the things you cannot control and gain power over your life. Stay calm – it is your superpower.

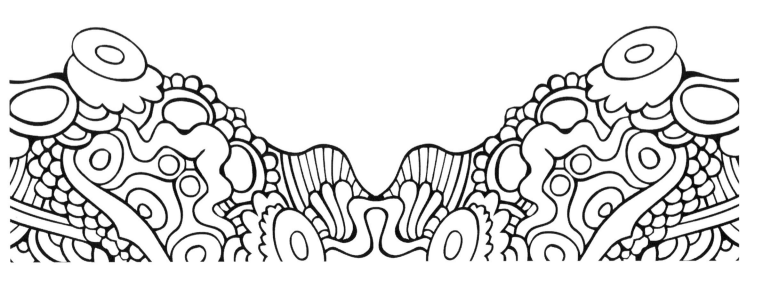

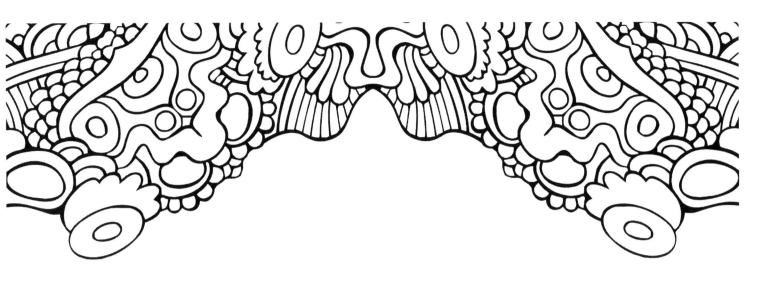

DISCOVER

Each day a new part of you is revealed.

Pay attention, the discovery never stops.

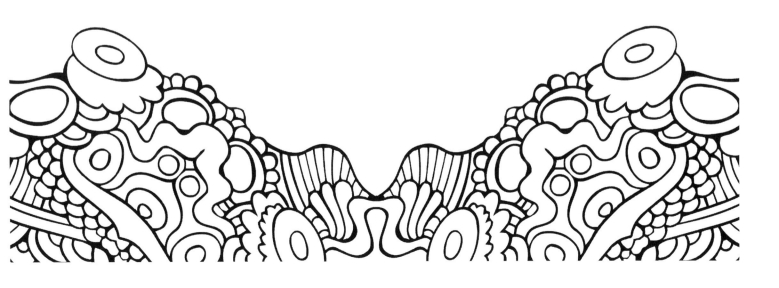

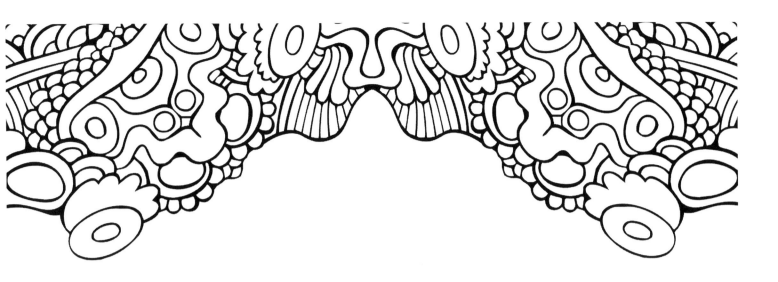

EMBRACE

Life is an endless journey of surprises.

Don't run from it.

Embrace life and it will embrace you.

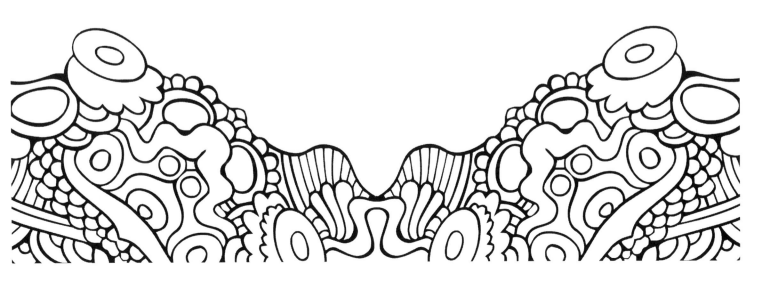

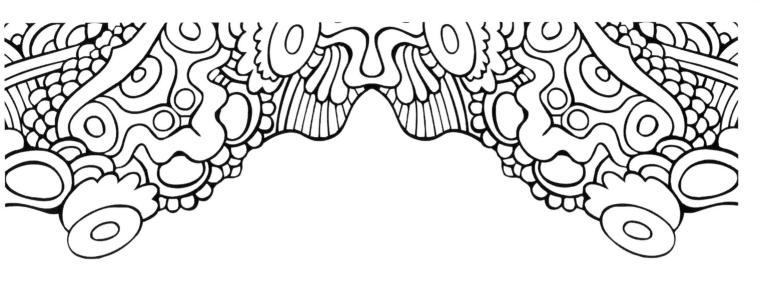

FREE

It's your life! You're the boss.

Let your true self rejoice by giving yourself

permission to be free in your thoughts, words, and actions.

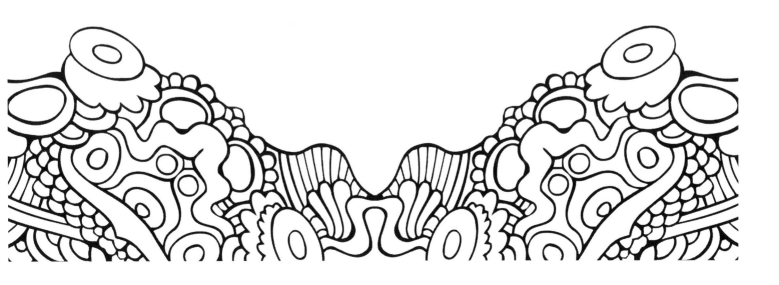

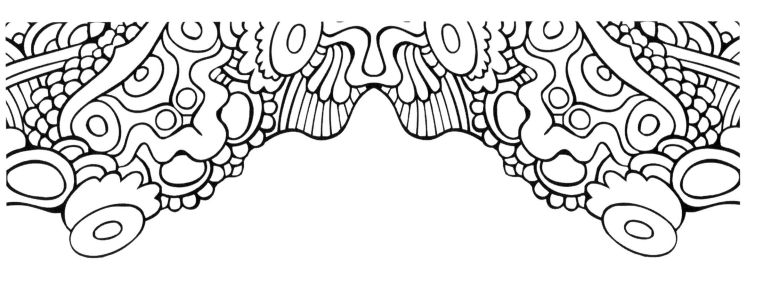

GRATITUDE

Gratitude gives you the authority to turn an

ordinary day into an amazing experience.

Seeing the good in all things makes life incredible.

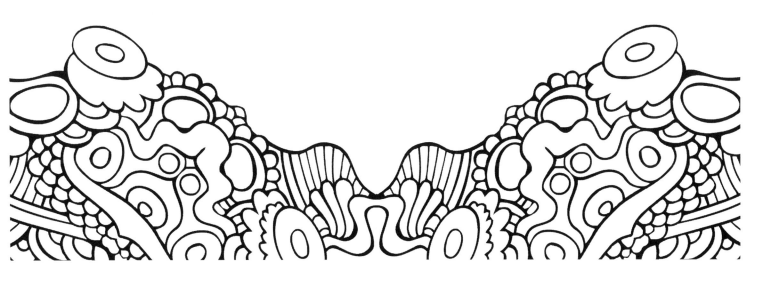

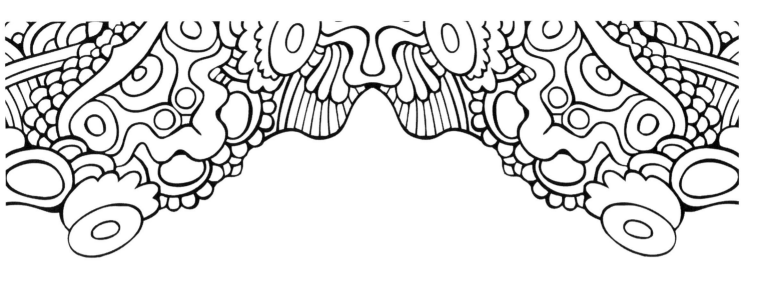

HARMONY

Harmony happens when your beliefs, thoughts,

words, and actions align.

It's when your heart and mind finally agree.

Give yourself room to express your true self and

harmony will follow.

Be at peace with your uniqueness.

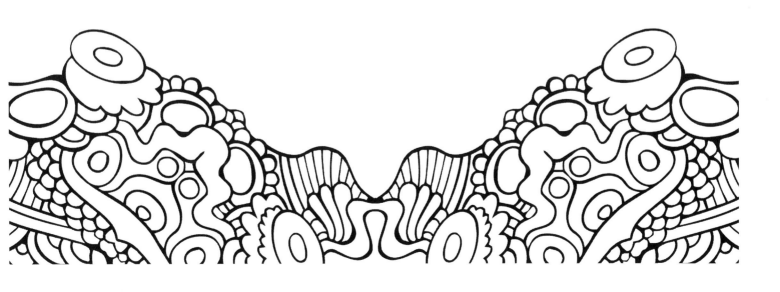

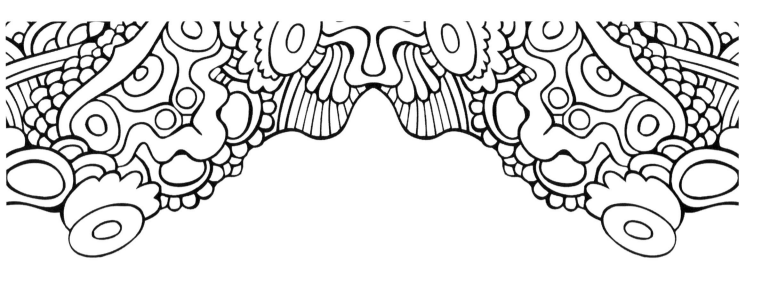

INTENTIONAL

Positivity isn't created by accident, it is intentional.

Choosing to live with intention instead of

habit is the one of the first steps to changing your life.

Live intentionally.

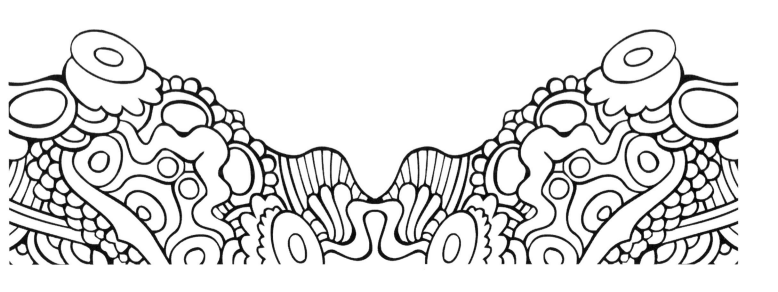

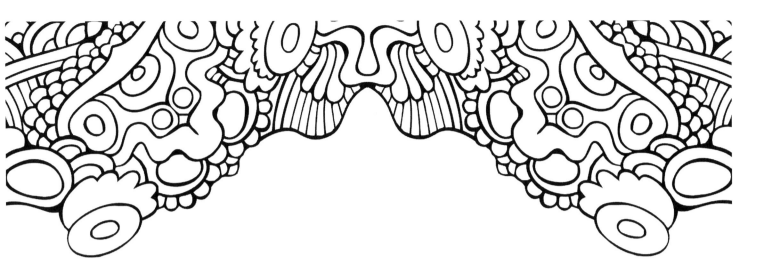

JOY

Never just focus on the destination, it is the process

that teaches you the most. Appreciate the process;

for the secret to finding joy is learning how to find the

value in all things and appreciating it.

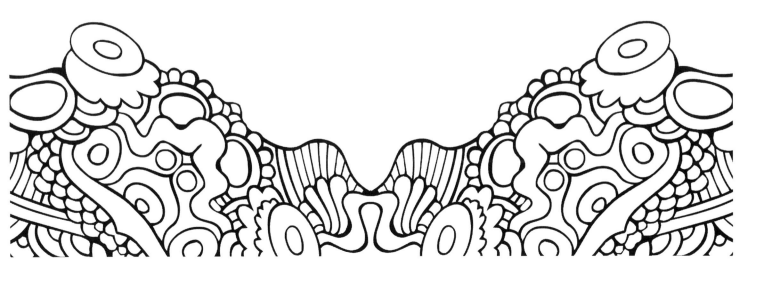

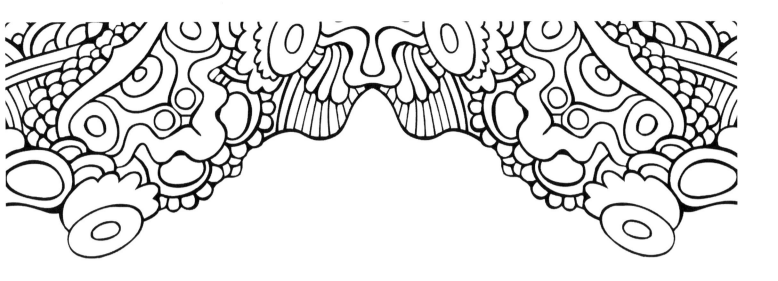

KINDNESS

Kindness is the universal language. The deaf and blind

can understand it and the numb can feel it.

It draws the best out of us. Be kind to yourself.

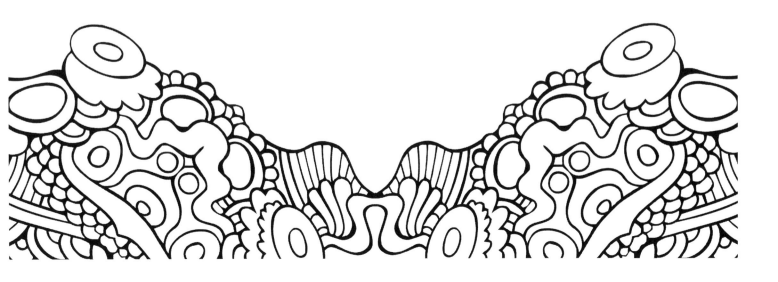

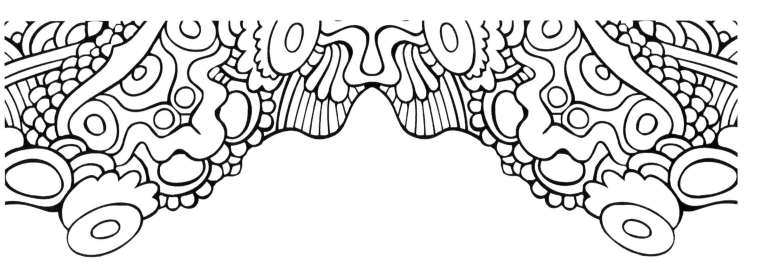

LAUGH

Laugh more and worry less. If laughing is contagious

make it an epidemic.

Have a dose of laughter and let it heal your soul

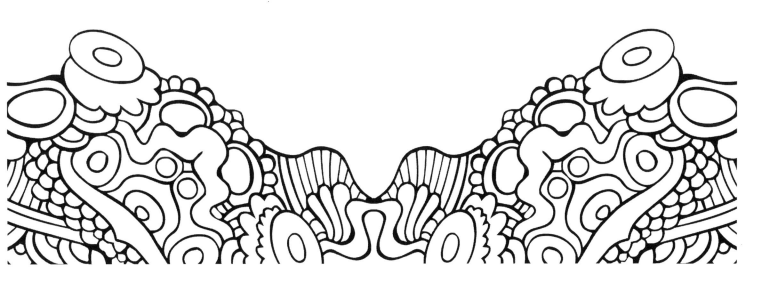

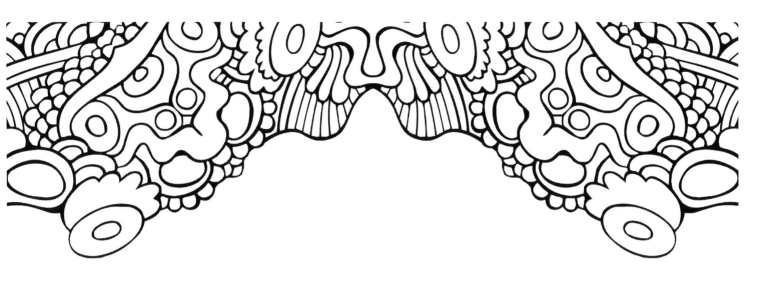

MINDFUL

Life gives us gifts wrapped up in moments.

It's important that you are mindful of the moments

life grants you or you will miss the gift every time.

Take a deep breath, slow things down a little,

and pay attention to the world around you.

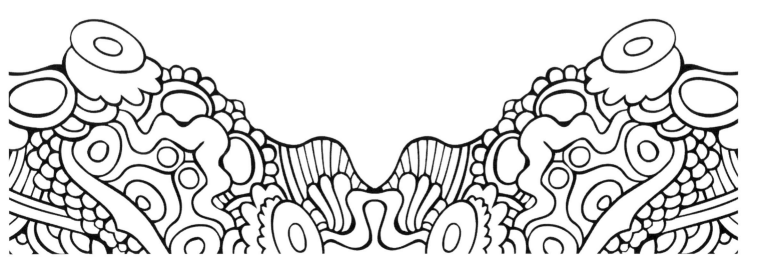

NO

Boundaries are a necessity and saying NO

helps to reinforce them.

The word NO is a complete sentence.

It's ok to say NO.

OPTIMISTIC

Optimism is vital to accomplishment and happiness.

Look at the bright side of things and watch

problems quickly turn into opportunities.

Be optimistic.

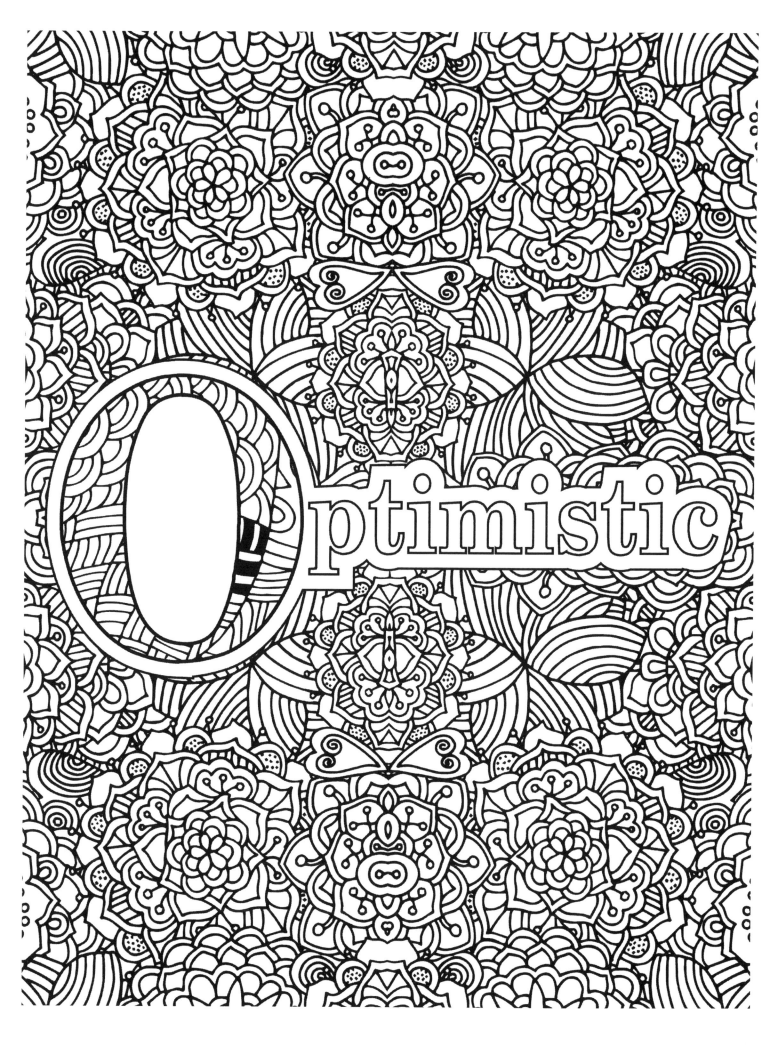

PRIORITY

Life is about priorities.

What you prioritize subliminally tells

others what you value most.

Make yourself a priority and others will,

too. There is power in prioritization.

QUIETNESS

The loudest things are often spoken in quietness.

Allow your mind to rest and your soul will speak.

Still away for some quiet time.

Your mind will thank you.

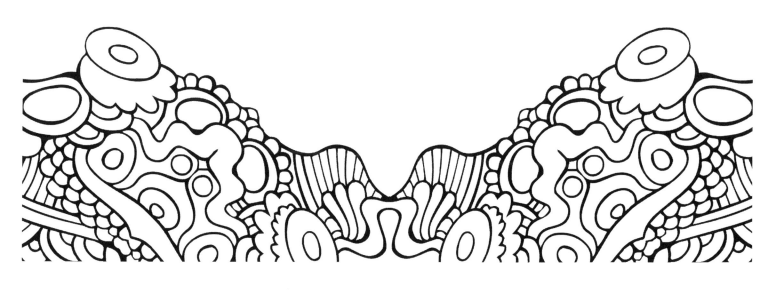

REPLENISH

You serve best when you are replenished and full.

Keep your cup full; stay connected to your

source of inspiration and motivation.

It's difficult to serve others on empty.

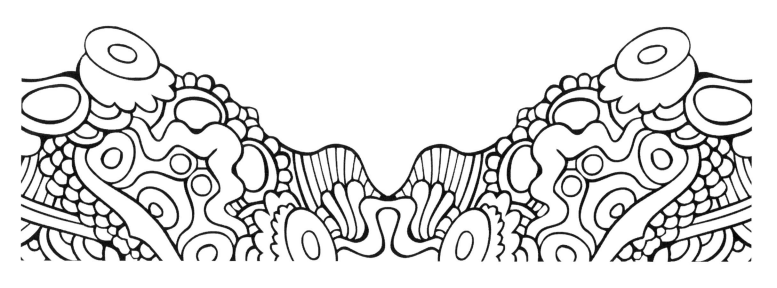

SMILE

Smiles are a symbol of beauty.

A smile can add beauty to even the

most unpleasant situations.

Regardless of what you may face today smile

and give it your best shot.

Knock it out with a smile.

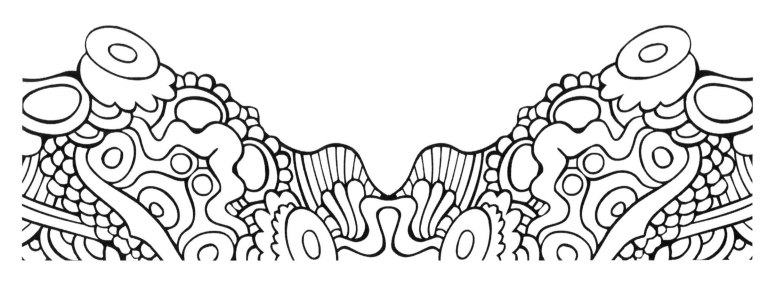

TIME

Time is one of your most precious commodities

and you should spend it on your most prized possession,

YOU.

Make time for you.

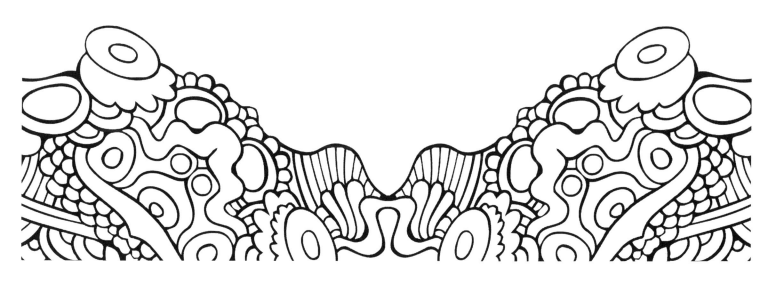

UPLIFT

What you do for others inevitably reciprocates itself.

Make it your mission to uplift someone. Encourage

them and compliment them on purpose.

He who uplifts others will, themselves, be uplifted.

VALUE

Values exist to be acknowledged, not ignored.

Honoring your values helps you to live a

more meaningful and productive life.

WORTH

When you truly understand your worth,

you will not discount yourself.

Rarities are never discounted.

Self-care is a necessity and you are worth the investment.

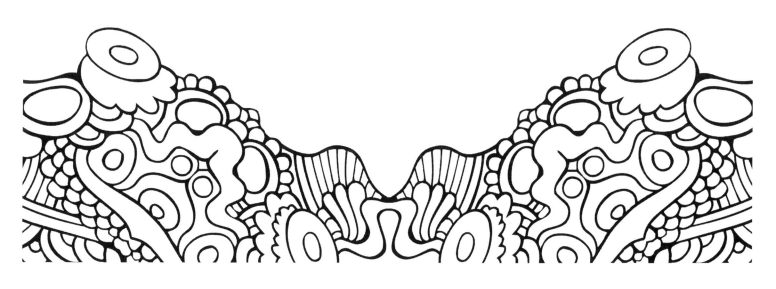

X- FACTOR

It is impossible to be good at everything, but you are

uniquely great at something. We all have special talents

and virtues that make us extraordinary; your x-factor.

Your x-factor is a gift to you but for others to enjoy.

Identify it and nurture it because the world needs it.

YIELD

Yielding does not promote weakness, but strength.

When you learn to flow with the moments life grants you,

you achieve a greater awareness and appreciation for life.

ZEAL

Never underestimate the power of zeal.

Zeal is what fuels you daily,

as long as you cherish and cultivate it you are unstoppable.

ABOUT THE AUTHOR

Terricka Hardy, LCSW, ACSW, BCD is a Licensed Clinical Social Worker, member of the national Academy of Certified Social Workers, Board Certified Diplomate in Clinical Social Work, therapist, and national presenter and speaker.

Her area of expertise is comprised of burnout prevention and resiliency, ethics, self-care awareness, and mental health recovery. Terricka has worked with individuals from many walks of life such as chronically ill adults, individuals at high risk for suicide, and children who have been abused and/or neglected. She is an appointed member of the National Association of Social Workers (NASW) Ethics Committee and recently partnered with NASW to rewrite and revise the NASW policy statement on professional impairment. Terricka is passionate about helping others achieve emotional wellness and has presented on self-care awareness at the local, state, and national levels.

She truly believes that self-care is the best care.

CONTACT:
Email: thardylcsw@yahoo.com
Facebook: https://www.facebook.com/thardylcsw
LinkedIn: https://www.linkedin.com/in/terricka-hardy-678298101

Share your beautiful and creative coloring pages, from this book, with the author by emailing a picture of your work to thardylcsw@yahoo.com.

Made in the USA
San Bernardino, CA
12 September 2017